Men, Women and Children
in
The First World War

Philip Steele

WAYLAND

Published in 2013 by Wayland

Copyright © Wayland 2013

Wayland
338 Euston Road
London NW1 3BH

Wayland
Level 17/207 Kent Street
Sydney, NSW 2000

British Library Cataloguing in Publication Data
Steele, Philip, 1948-
  Men, women and children in the First World War.
  1. World War, 1914-1918--Social aspects--Juvenile literature. 2. World War, 1914-1918--
Social aspects--Great Britain--Juvenile literature. 3. Great Britain--History--George V, 1910-1936--
Juvenile literature.
  I. Title
  940.3-dc22
  ISBN: 978 0 7502 7192 9

Printed in China

Wayland is a division of Hachette Children's Books, an Hachette UK Company.
www.hachette.co.uk

Picture acknowledgments: akg-images/Alamy: 22; Bentley Archive/Popperfoto/Getty Images:
Cover (BL), 25; Mary Evans Picture Library: 4, 14, 16, 24; Firmin/Hulton Archive/Getty Images: 13
Tim Graham/Getty Images: 27; The Granger Collection/Topfoto/TopFoto.co.uk: 19, 26; David J.
Green/Alamy: Cover (Main), 8; Hulton Archive/Getty Images: 17; Map Studio: 6; Pictorial Press
Ltd/Alamy: 23; The Print Collector/Alamy: 15; Jimmy Sime/Hulton Archive/Getty Images: 9; ©
Swim Ink, LLC/Corbis: 10; Thislife Pictures/Alamy: 18 Topfoto/TopFoto.co.uk: 7; ©2003 Topham/
Picturepoint/TopFoto.co.uk: 20; Topical Press Agency/Hulton Archive/Getty Images: Cover (LC), 5,
12, 21; John Warwick Brooke/Hulton Archive/Getty Images: Cover (TL), Title page, 11

CONTENTS

WHAT WAS THE FIRST WORLD WAR?   6

MEN, WOMEN AND CHILDREN   8

WHAT WAS IT LIKE TO GO TO WAR?   10

WHAT WAS IT LIKE TO STAY AT HOME?   12

WHAT DID PEOPLE EAT DURING THE WAR YEARS?   14

HOW DID PEOPLE DRESS IN WARTIME?   16

WHAT WAS SCHOOL LIKE DURING THE FIRST WORLD WAR?   18

WHAT WORK DID PEOPLE DO?   20

HOW DID PEOPLE HAVE FUN DESPITE THE WAR?   22

WHAT DID PEOPLE THINK ABOUT THE WAR?   24

WHAT HAPPENED WHEN THE WAR ENDED?   26

GLOSSARY   28

FURTHER INFORMATION   29

INDEX   30

Words that appear in **bold**
can be found in the glossary
on page 28.

WHAT WAS THE FIRST WORLD WAR?

Between 1914 and 1918 there was a terrible war. More than 9.7 million troops and over 8.9 million civilians were killed. The soldiers came from Europe, Asia, Africa, North America and the Caribbean, Australia and New Zealand. At the time this was called 'the Great War'. When a second global conflict broke out between 1939 and 1945, the Great War became known as 'the First World War', or 'World War I'.

BEFORE THE WAR

In 1900 many people greeted the new century with hope. They looked forward to a new age of progress, to better living conditions and new scientific discoveries. Everyday life seemed well ordered. In reality, however, the world was becoming a more dangerous place. There was fierce rivalry between the nations in Europe. Germany was building itself up as an aggressive military power. Great Britain was building deadly new battleships. European nations ruled large overseas empires. They sometimes fought with each other over these territories.

Central Powers 1914.
Neutral countries later aligned with Central Powers.
Allies 1914.
Neutral countires later aligned with Allies.
Allied with Central Powers, declared neutrality at outbreak of war, then joined Allies.
Countries remaining neutral.

▲ This map shows how some countries joined with Great Britain and the Allies and others joined with Germany and the Central Powers during the course of the war.

THE WORLD WAR ONE TIMELINE

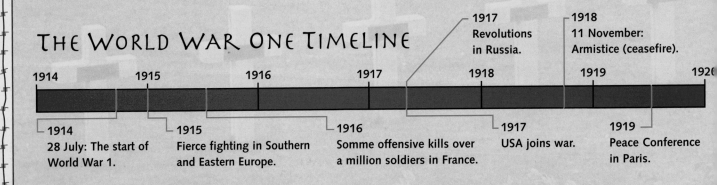

1917
Revolutions in Russia.

1918
11 November: Armistice (ceasefire).

| 1914 | 1915 | 1916 | 1917 | 1918 | 1919 | 1920 |

1914
28 July: The start of World War 1.

1915
Fierce fighting in Southern and Eastern Europe.

1916
Somme offensive kills over a million soldiers in France.

1917
USA joins war.

1919
Peace Conference in Paris.

> "WE ARE FIGHTING FOR A WORTHY PURPOSE AND WE SHALL NOT LAY DOWN OUR ARMS UNTIL THAT PURPOSE HAS BEEN ACHIEVED."
>
> *The King.*

▲ As Britain entered the war, this message from the King was displayed in Trafalgar Square, in central London. As the war progressed, newspaper journalists and pro-war politicians on both sides tried to whip up hatred against the enemy.

WAR BREAKS OUT

The world's most powerful nations had tried to prevent conflict by drawing up a series of agreements between nations. However when trouble did break out, these agreements only served to drag one country after another into war. On 28 June 1914, in Sarajevo, a Serbian student shot dead Archduke Franz Ferdinand, the heir to the Austrian throne. This led to Austria-Hungary declaring war on Serbia. In the months and years that followed, 32 nations lined up on one side or the other.

TIMES OF CHANGE

World War 1 killed more people than any conflict before it in the history of the world. After the war, nothing remained the same. What was it like to live through these extraordinary times? How were people affected by warfare and hardship?

MEN, WOMEN AND CHILDREN

Fewer people lived in Europe a hundred years ago. Britain and Ireland had a population of about 42 million, compared with about 63 million today. There were great differences between rich and poor, and society was strictly divided into social classes. Voting rights were still limited, so most people had little control over how they were governed or sent off to war. Landowners were very powerful, and the Churches too had great influence over people's everyday lives.

▲ A typical British family of the period poses for the camera. Perhaps the eldest son is about to leave for the war.

A MAN'S WORLD

Men were regarded as the head of the family. It was they who were responsible for money matters and for making important decisions. They were not expected to help with household duties, and would never have been seen cleaning the house or cooking. Men controlled the world of politics and economics. When they went off to war between 1914 and 1918, it greatly affected family life and the world of work.

WOMEN IN THE 1900s

In wealthy families, women ran the household and supervised servants. In less well off families, women looked after the children, cooked and cleaned, and often worked long hours as servants, or in factories and mills. They were poorly paid. During the war, women took on jobs that had previously been done only by men.

GROWING UP

Families were larger than today, with an average of three or four children. Discipline at home was strict, but children in wealthy families enjoyed comfortable surroundings and good food. Conditions for poor children had improved since the 1800s, but many still lived in badly built, damp housing, and had a poor diet.

REAL LIVES

EMMELINE PANKHURST, SUFFRAGETTE

Emmeline Pankhurst (1858-1928) was born in Manchester, England. She and her daughters campaigned for women's suffrage (the right to vote). From 1903 Emmeline and her '**suffragettes**' used extreme methods of protest, such as breaking windows. Emmeline supported the war in 1914, and halted her suffrage campaign. However the war did change attitudes towards women. In 1918 British women over 30 years of age were given the vote. All men and women gained equal voting rights in 1929.

▶ Emmeline Pankhurst is carried away from a protest in London before the war. The suffragettes were often jailed and had to brave public anger and ridicule.

WHAT WAS IT LIKE TO GO TO WAR?

In August 1914 young men on both sides of the conflict volunteered to join the armed forces. They marched through the streets to the sound of cheers and patriotic songs. Everyone said the war would be over by Christmas, but people soon realised that this would be a longer, more desperate struggle. **Conscription** of soldiers, which made all younger men liable for military service, was introduced in Britain for the first time early in 1916. Many women enrolled as nurses or ambulance drivers.

THE LONG ORDEAL

On the **Western Front**, neither side could gain an advantage. Soon two lines of **trenches** and barbed wire stretched all the way from the North Sea to the Swiss border. Between them lay a strip of mud, filled with **shell** holes and raked by gunfire. Troops would cross this **no-man's-land** to launch attacks on the enemy's trenches. They died in their thousands to win a few hundred metres of territory, only to lose it again in the following weeks.

WOMEN OF BRITAIN SAY – "GO!"

▲ A recruitment poster. Sometimes women handed out white feathers to those men who had not yet joined up, as a symbol of cowardice.

THE FRONT LINE

Life and death on the Western Front was grim. The trenches were filled with mud and water, and overrun with rats. Discipline was harsh. The soldiers were exhausted, often sick or driven out of their minds by **shell shock**. Many showed great bravery trying to rescue their wounded comrades, or just surviving.

MODERN WARFARE

Terrible new ways of waging war were used during World War 1. These included submarines, tanks, aircraft, gigantic guns and poison gas, which blinded and choked the victims.

▶ A wounded soldier is carried on a stretcher during the slaughter at Passchendaele, in Flanders. On both sides of the conflict, the troops suffered terribly.

REAL LIVES

HARRY PATCH, THE LAST 'TOMMY'

Harry Patch (1898-2009) was born in Somerset, England. He left school in 1913 and trained to be a plumber. He was conscripted, and in 1917 was wounded at Passchendaele, in a battle that took the lives of 570,000 soldiers. Afterwards, Harry would not discuss his wartime experiences. Only in old age did he speak out about the horrors of war and his desire for a peaceful world. Harry lived to be 111 years old, the last surviving 'Tommy' (British soldier) from the trenches.

WHAT WAS IT LIKE TO STAY AT HOME?

Back at home, **civilians** tried to carry on with their lives as normal. Women and children supported the war effort by knitting mittens or scarves for the troops, or sending out bandages to the hospitals. There was constant anxiety about loved ones who were away fighting. People could read newspaper reports of battles, but in the days before radio broadcasts or television it was impossible to imagine the real conditions at the front. When soldiers came home on leave, they did not like to admit their fears, or worry their families with the harsh reality.

▲ A wealthy lady of the house and her cook demonstrate how to use potatoes and rice in place of flour, which was in short supply during the First World War.

OUT AND ABOUT

On city streets many men now wore military uniforms. Railway stations were thronged with troops, but everyday life had to continue. Buses and trams carried office workers, or shoppers visiting department stores. Bicycles were popular, but motor cars were still expensive to own. Steam trains carried passengers to the recently built suburbs. In the high streets, grocers' shops windows displayed advertisements for tea, matches, tobacco or soap. Home deliveries of groceries, bread or laundry continued, using horse-drawn wagons.

COMMUNITY SUPPORT

People often remained living in the districts in which they had been brought up. Although people were more formal with each other than today, support was offered by these close community and family ties. The war affected almost every home, from the great country estates of the aristocracy, whose sons served as army officers, to the rural cottages of farm labourers, from the red-brick terraces housing factory workers, to city slums. As casualties mounted, almost everyone knew families who had suffered.

▶ 'Put 'em up!' Poor boys from the slums of Shadwell, a district in London, stage a boxing match in the street for their friends.

REAL LIVES

DAVID LLOYD GEORGE, PRIME MINISTER

David Lloyd George (1863-1945) was a Welsh lawyer who became a Liberal Member of Parliament in the UK. He served as Chancellor from 1912-1915 and brought in the first Old Age Pensions. In 1916 he became Prime Minister and was an effective wartime leader. After the war, he promised to build new housing 'fit for heroes' – but economic problems soon ended his plans.

WHAT DID PEOPLE EAT DURING THE WAR YEARS?

Horses hauled wagons of supplies and mobile **field kitchens** to the soldiers on the front line. The troops were issued with food **rations** such as meat, bacon, cheese, tea, bread, jam and vegetables, as well as rum and tobacco. For British troops the most common meal was tinned corned beef, known as 'bully beef'. At times food ran short or supplies were spoiled by rats. Water was often foul, causing illnesses such as **dysentery**.

▲ A poster calls on people to save food. U-boats were German submarines which attacked shipping carrying food and supplies to Britain.

IN THE KITCHEN

In the 1900s, food and eating habits varied greatly between nations, regions and classes. Poor people could afford only the most basic meals, and **malnutrition** was common. In better-off households the whole family would sit down to eat large meals at the same times each day. Tinned foods were common, but refrigerators were not yet used in the home.

SUPPLIES AND STARVATION

Britain's Royal Navy had **blockaded** Germany's North Sea ports from the start of the war, and the land war too halted supplies into Germany. The lack of food in Germany was severe and by the end of the war hundreds of thousands of civilians had died of starvation. In Britain, food shortages also began to affect the civilian population. German submarines or U-boats sank many ships carrying supplies from overseas.

PRODUCE AND RATIONING

Encouraged to grow their own food, people dug vegetable plots on commons and in parks. In Britain the Women's Land Army recruited thousands of women to help with the work on farms. The Women's Institute, founded in 1915, taught women about producing and preserving food in wartime. Rationing of foods such as sugar and meat was introduced, to prevent 'panic buying' and ensure that everyone had enough to eat.

▲ King George V admires home-grown vegetables on London's Clapham Common, which has been turned into allotments for growing food.

REAL LIVES

AUGUSTE ESCOFFIER, CHEF

Georges Auguste Escoffier (1846-1935) was a great French chef, who ruled the kitchens in London's grand Carlton Hotel. At the start of World War 1, two-thirds of his staff left for the war and he struggled to find enough meat, fish and other supplies. However he still managed to produce meals for his rich and famous customers. One of Escoffier's sons, serving with the French army, was killed in 1914. The chef raised funds for the welfare of Allied soldiers and their families.

HOW DID PEOPLE DRESS IN WARTIME?

During World War 1, front line troops of all armies wore the dull colours needed to protect them from enemy rifle fire. Uniforms were khaki, grey or blue. Boots and leg bindings called **puttees** protected against the mud. Officers wore high leather boots, a shoulder strap and belt of polished leather, with a holster for a pistol. Steel helmets were worn during fighting, saving many lives.

MEN'S CIVVIES

'Civvies' (civilian clothes) for men varied greatly according to class. Everyone wore hats in public – flat caps, bowler hats, brimmed felt hats or round straw 'boaters'. Formal suits were worn more generally than now, and were essential for office work or church on Sunday.

▲ Hats, suits and dresses... Note the variety of fashions on display in this crowd on the edge of Hyde Park, in London.

WOMEN'S COSTUME

The big hats worn by women at the turn of the century gave way to smaller hats (often with one or two straight feathers), or round hats with a broad brim. Dresses and overcoats were ankle-length at the start of the war, but hems were raised to mid-calf level by 1916. Shoes, generally with a low heel, began to replace button boots as footwear. During the war, womens' dress became simpler and the wartime needs of working women resulted in more practical fashions. Women began to cut their hair shorter and even wear trousers for manual labour.

WE ARE NOT DOWNHEARTED.

▶ A World War I propaganda postcard shows a little girl leading boys dressed in the uniforms of the Allied forces – Russia, Belgium, France and Britain.

CHILDREN'S CLOTHES

In the 1900s families liked to have their pictures taken in photographers' studios. Many soldiers carried photos of their children with them to the front. During the war, boys began to wear more informal, active clothes, such as woollen jumpers, knee-length shorts and long socks. Girls might wear pinafore dresses (sometimes with a 'sailor-suit' collar) and ankle boots.

REAL LIVES

CHARLIE CHAPLIN, FILM STAR

Charlie Chaplin (1889-1977) was born in London. A natural comic and performer, he became the first film star to be known worldwide. From 1914 his most famous comedy act was dressed as a little tramp, wearing a bowler hat, a crumpled suit, old boots and carrying a cane. In the 1918 film *Shoulder Arms*, Chaplin clowned around in uniform on the Western Front.

WHAT WAS SCHOOL LIKE DURING THE FIRST WORLD WAR?

The effects of World War 1 were felt in schools all over Europe. Many schoolmasters left to join the armed forces and were replaced in the classroom by women teachers. Teachers sometimes read out tales of heroism, or newspaper reports about the progress of the war. On both sides of the conflict, children were encouraged to be patriotic. In the playground there was great interest in warships and air battles.

IN THE CLASSROOM

A typical village or town school in Britain had separate entrances for boys and girls. Assembly would begin with prayers. Classrooms had rows of wooden desks facing a blackboard, and on the wall there might be large map of the world, with the various empires and nations shown in different colours. Teachers kept strict discipline, and punishments might include a caning, a rap across the hand, or a detention.

LEARNING AND WRITING

Small children learned to write with chalk on a slate, before moving on to **copy books** and pencils, and then to pen and ink. Much time was spent learning off by heart the rules of spelling and grammar, doing sums, or learning the names of rivers, oceans and capital cities.

▼ This is a typical British schoolroom at the start of World War I. The children sit at neat wooden desks, watched over by women teachers.

PUBLIC SCHOOLS AND OFFICERS

The officers in the First World War were mostly recruited from the middle and upper classes. Education at Britain's influential public schools (actually private schools) was very different from the council-run elementary schools. Lessons included Latin, Greek, science and advanced mathematics and great emphasis was placed on sport and toughness. Junior Officer Training Corps (OTCs) were founded to introduce pupils to weapons training, drilling and exercises before they left school.

REAL LIVES

WILFRED OWEN, POET

Wilfred Owen (1893-1918) was born in Shropshire, England. He worked as teacher before becoming a junior officer in 1916. Wilfred was one of the war's greatest English-language poets, describing the terrible waste of young lives. He suffered from severe shell shock, and returned to Britain for treatment. He returned to the Western Front in 1918, but was killed just one week before the end of the war.

▶ Wilfred Owen wrote of young men being slaughtered like cattle and the 'monstrous anger of the guns'.

WHAT WORK DID PEOPLE DO?

The industrial age was at its height in the early 1900s. The leading nations in World War 1 were great manufacturers, producing coal, steel, ships, textiles, armaments and chemicals. Chimneys belched out smoke over industrial areas. Factory hours were long, accidents were common and wages were low. Campaigners were working to improve conditions.

WOMEN IN FACTORIES

When the men went off to war, women took over many of their heavy labouring jobs. They heaved sacks of coal at power stations. They became welders and worked at shipyards, at glass factories or chemical works. They spent long hours making ammunition for the big guns on the Western Front.

SERVICE JOBS

During the First World War women took on more service jobs, for example working in offices and banks. Of course many men were still working, including those too young or old to be conscripted, those unfit for fighting and those, such as doctors and farmers, whose jobs were essential to keep things going.

THESE WOMEN ARE DOING THEIR BIT

LEARN TO MAKE MUNITIONS

▶ A propaganda poster shows a female munitions worker pulling on her overalls, as a male worker marches off to war.

ON THE LAND

During the war, the number of British women working on the land doubled. Farms at this time used steam for threshing, but still relied largely on horses to pull machines such as ploughs. Women had always helped out on the farm, but now they took on all sorts of work, from harvesting to forestry.

▶ In the spring of 1917, these three women are ploughing up waste ground owned by London's Metropolitan Railway, in order to plant potatoes.

REAL LIVES

MARIE CURIE, SCIENTIST

Marie Curie (1867-1934) was one of the most famous scientists in history. She was born in Poland, but went to France to study. In 1903 and 1911 she won Nobel Prizes in physics and chemistry. During World War 1 Marie and her daughter Irène fitted out and drove lorries containing newly developed X-ray equipment. The two women had to argue with generals to gain access to front line hospitals. They taught medical officers how to take X-rays, and saved the lives of countless wounded soldiers.

HOW DID PEOPLE HAVE FUN DESPITE THE WAR?

The front line soldiers, though exhausted, found time to read a letter from home or play a tune on the mouth organ. The troops developed a sharp sense of humour, despite their wretched living conditions. When marching back to the shell-battered towns and villages behind the lines, they would sing hymns or the popular songs of the day, often making up comic or rude versions to poke fun at their own officers, or the enemy.

◀ German troops find time for a game of football in 1917. At the start of the war, German, British and French troops were recorded as climbing out of the trenches to play football with each other, in order to celebrate Christmas.

MUSIC HALL AND CINEMA

The popular places of entertainment in the cities were known in Britain as music halls. These would stage variety shows including songs, comedy acts and dances. Music hall stars played a part in keeping up **morale** during wartime, calling on men in the audience to join the army. The very latest in entertainment was the cinema. Films were still silent and in black-and-white, with music provided by a piano player.

HOME ENTERTAINMENTS

At home there were no public radio broadcasts, and television was unknown. Wind-up phonographs played music recorded on to cylinders, and flat records becoming popular too. Pianos took pride of place in many homes, and families would gather around them for a 'sing-song'. Card and board games were popular, and some of these were based on issues of the day, such as votes for women.

GAMES AND TOYS

Children enjoyed traditional games such as leapfrog or hopscotch, or playing with model boats. Teddy bears had been first made in 1903, and children also played with metal toys. Models of motor buses and vans, battleships and airships were popular. Germany was the world's biggest toy manufacturer, but because of the war people on the side of the Allies did not buy German products.

OUTDOOR ACTIVITIES

Sports became hugely popular in the 1900s. In Britain, people loved cycling and boating, watching football or cricket or playing lawn tennis. Discussion about football teams was a constant topic of conversation in the trenches. However matches were virtually shut down in Britain during the war years.

REAL LIVES

MARIE LLOYD, ENTERTAINER

Marie Lloyd (1870-1922) was a Londoner and one of the most popular stars of the English music hall. Her best-loved songs were romantic or comic, and often a bit cheeky. During the war Marie encouraged men to join the army, and gave free concerts to wounded soldiers returning from the Western Front.

WHAT DID PEOPLE THINK ABOUT THE WAR?

Opinions about the war varied greatly, depending on people's political views, religious beliefs, ideals, nationality and personal experiences. The original enthusiasm for the war faded as the fighting took its toll. Many people were concerned about the way in which the generals' plans led to such massive loss of life. Anger about the slaughter was expressed clearly in the works of poets and artists. Many people were also worried that the massive cost of the war was draining away the wealth of their nation.

FOR THE WAR

Most of the large political parties across Europe came to support the war as a matter of national pride or gain. When the USA joined the war in 1917, it declared that the fight was for **democracy** against **autocracy** (rule by a powerful emperor, such as Kaiser Wilhelm II). This idea was widely accepted among the Allies. However Russia, the biggest country on the Allied side, was itself ruled by an autocrat, Tsar Nicholas II, and on neither side were there fully democratic governments.

◄ This propaganda photograph shows the Allies as a noble, happy band of brothers. The reality was very different. During World War I there were disputes on all sides, mutinies and even uprisings and revolutions.

AGAINST THE WAR

Some people objected to the war on moral or religious grounds. **Pacifist** groups were founded, such as the Women's International League for Peace and Freedom (WILPF). Quakers believed that their Christian faith did not permit them to kill other human beings. They would only agree to carry stretchers or drive ambulances at the front. Many **conscientious objectors**, who refused to join the forces, were sent to jail.

◄ Opposition grew as the war dragged on. These peace campaigners and conscientious objectors are meeting at Devon, in England, in 1917.

REAL LIVES

BERTRAND RUSSELL, PHILOSOPHER

Bertrand Russell (1872-1970) was a leading **philosopher** and mathematician. From the start, Russell claimed that the war was madness, based on narrow national interests and the pride of political leaders. He supported those who refused to fight, and was removed from his post at Cambridge University because of his views. In 1918 he was sent to prison.

WHAT HAPPENED WHEN THE WAR ENDED?

The fighting ended on 11 November 1918, at 11am. Germany had signed an **armistice**, or ceasefire agreement. The big guns fell silent. The soldiers on the front were in a state of disbelief. In all the Allied countries, crowds of men, women and children poured onto the streets, cheering, waving flags, singing and dancing. In Germany there was relief, but also hunger and anger as the Kaiser or emperor was forced from power.

THE SEARCH FOR PEACE

A long peace conference was held in Paris in 1919. The defeated nations were not allowed to take part, and much of the agreement only served to create further political troubles. Some of these led directly to the horrors of the Second World War (1939-45). The Paris conference did result in the setting up of an international treaty organisation, the League of Nations, which was forerunner of the United Nations.

▶ Allied troops and French civilians celebrate the Armistice on the streets of Paris, on 11 November 1918.

SOCIAL CHANGES

After World War 1, the way people lived changed greatly. Some of the old differences between social classes began to wear away. Women gained the vote in many countries. Many men and women simply tried to forget the war years. They wanted to dance, listen to jazz, drive cars and wear daring fashions. However in the 1920s and 30s a great economic depression caused hardship around the world. Many people lost their money or their jobs, and went hungry. Many of the dreams that had looked so promising in 1918 did not happen.

REMEMBRANCE

Graves now stretched over the fields near where the war had been fought. Row upon row of white crosses showed that a whole generation of young men had been lost. Of those who survived, many were left disabled, blind or confused. The terrible cost of the First World War continues to trouble the world to this day. Remembrance services are still held each year on 11 November. In Britain, the symbol of remembrance is a poppy, like the ones that grew over the fields of the Western Front.

▲ Young boys carry a wreath of poppies to commemorate the war dead, in London in 2007.

Glossary

armistice: laying down arms at the end of a war, calling off hostilities

autocracy: rule by a single, powerful monarch or despot

blockade: using warships to prevent enemy ships leaving ports or trading freely

civilian: a citizen who is not a member of the armed forces

civvies: civilian clothes, not military uniform

conscientious objector: someone who refuses to fight as a matter of conscience or principle

conscription: ordering people to join the armed forces

copy books: books used to teach handwriting with examples to copy

democracy: rule by the people or by representatives of the people

dysentery: an illness of the intestine, causing diarrhoea and bleeding

empire: a group of different lands and territories ruled by a single government

field kitchen: wagons or trucks used to heat up or prepare food for front line troops

malnutrition: medical problems caused by a shortage of healthy food

morale: the way people feel about a war and if they believe their side can win

no-man's-land: the strip of land between two hostile enemies, or between the borders of two countries

pacifist: someone who campaigns for peace and rejects all violence

philosopher: someone who studies ideas and the rights and wrongs of human behaviour

puttees: strips of cloth wound around the leg as part of military uniform, used as protection and support

rations: the food issued to troops while in action

shell: explosive ammunition for big guns

shell shock: stress disorder brought about by the trauma of combat and shelling

suffragette: a campaigner for women's right to vote

trench: a long, narrow pit dug from the soil to protect a line of troops

Western Front: the battle lines in Western Europe between opposing sides in the First World War

Further Information

More books to read

Simon Adams
Eyewitness: World War I
(Dorling Kindersley, 2004)

Ruth Brocklehurst
and Henry Brook
**The Usborne Introduction to
the First World War**
(Usborne Publishing in
association with the
Imperial War Museum, 2007)

Ann Kramer
**Women and War:
World War One**
(Franklin Watts, 2004)

Michael Morpurgo
(fiction) **Private Peaceful**
(HarperCollins, 2004)

**The Penguin Book of First
World War Poetry**
(Penguin Classics, 2006)

Philip Steele
**Documenting History:
World War I**
(Wayland, 2009)

Valerie Wilding
(fiction) **Road to War (My
Story): A First World War
Girl's Diary 1916-17**
(Scholastic, 2008)

Useful websites

http://www.bbc.co.uk/schools/worldwarone/
You can hear stories of people who lived
through the First World War, look at photos
and read extracts from wartime diaries, letters
and newspapers at this website.

**http://www.spartacus.schoolnet.co.uk/
FWW.htm**
A website with links to topics to do with World
War One, such as the battles, the political and
military leaders and the Home Front.

www.firstworldwar.com
Read first-hand accounts from people who
took part in the war, such as soldiers, nurses
and religious officials.

http://www.iwm.org.uk/
The Imperial War Museum's website includes
descriptions of its First World War galleries.

Places to visit

Imperial War Museum, London
http://london.iwm.org.uk/

Imperial War Museum North (Manchester)
http://north.iwm.org.uk/

Museum of London
http://www.museumoflondon.org.uk/English/

London Transport Museum
http://www.ltmuseum.co.uk/

National Army Museum
http://www.national-army-museum.ac.uk/
exhibitions/worldWars/page2-1.shtml

The Tank Museum
http://www.tankmuseum.org/

INDEX

Numbers in **bold** indicate pictures.

aircraft 11
Allies 23, 24, **24**, 26
Archduke Franz Ferdinand 7
armistice 26
autocracy 24

Chaplin, Charlie 17
Church 8, 16
civilians 6, 14, **26**
clothes 16, 16, 17, **17**
community ties 13
conscientious objectors 25, **25**
conscription 10
Curie, Marie 21

democracy 24
discipline 9, 18

economics 8
Escoffier, Georges Auguste 15

factories 9, 20
family life 8
farms 15, 21, **21**
field kitchens 14
food 14, 15
front line 14, 16, 21, 26

games 22, 23
Germany 6, 14, 23, 26
guns 11

hospitals 12, 21
household duties 8, 9

illness 14

League of Nations 26
Lloyd George, David 13
Lloyd, Marie 23, **23**

morale 22
music halls 22, 23

no-man's-land 10

officers 13, 16, 19, 22
Owen, Wilfred 19, **19**

pacifists 25
Pankhurst, Emmeline 9, **9**
poison gas 11
politics 8
poor people 8, 9, 14
poppies 27, **27**
population 8

Quakers 25

rationing 14, 15

remembrance services 27, **27**
rich people 8, 9, 14
Russell, Bertrand 25

Second World War 6, 26
servants 9
schools 18, **18**, 19
shell shock 19
soldiers 6, 12, 14, 15, 17, 21, 22, **22**, 23, 26
sport 22, 23
submarines 11, 14
suffragettes 9

tanks 11
toys 23
transport 12
trenches 10, 11
troops 6, 12, 14, 16, 22, **26**

uniforms 16

voting rights 8, 9, 27

war effort 12
Western Front 10, 11, 17, 19, 20, 23, 27
Women's Institute 15
Women's Land Army 15
work 8, 16, 20, **20**, 21, 21

X-rays 21